EXPLORATION
AND
DISCOVERY

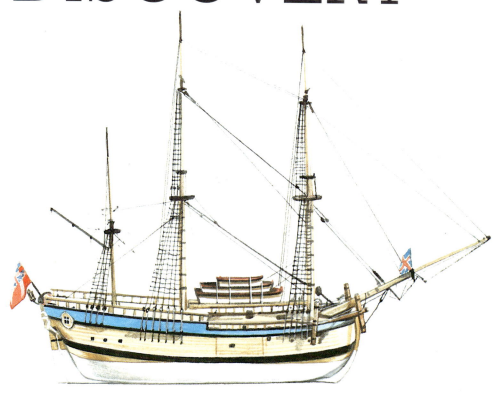

JOHN MAN

🪷 BELITHA PRESS

First published in Great Britain in 1990 by
Belitha Press Limited
31 Newington Green, London N16 9PU
Copyright © Belitha Press Limited and
Gareth Stevens, Inc. 1990
Illustrations/photographs copyright © in this
format by Belitha Press Limited and Gareth
Stevens, Inc. 1990
ISBN 1 85561 012 4
Reprinted 1991, 1992
Printed in Hong Kong for Imago

British Library Cataloguing in Publication Data
CIP data for this book is available from the British
Library

Acknowledgements

Photographic credits:

Bryan and Cherry Alexander 25 bottom
The Bodleian Library 24
Christian Bonington 59 top
Bridgeman Art Library 21 top
John Cleare/Mountain Camera 9, 13 top, 32/33,
    49 left, 51, 54 right, 55 centre
ET Archive 22, 23, 25 top left and right, 50 right
Mary Evans Picture Library 53 bottom, 54 left
Derek Fordham/Arctic Camera 57
Werner Forman Archive 15 bottom
Giraudon 27
Susan Griggs/Leon Schadeberg 6, /Victor
    Englebert 41 top, /Robert Azzi 46, /Anthony
    Howarth 47 top
Sonia Halliday 6 bottom
Robert Harding Picture Library 17, /George
    Douglass Brewerton: Crossing the Rocky
    Mountains, in the collection of The Corcoran
    Gallery of Art, Gift of William Wilson Corcoran
    29, /Schloss Tegel, East Berlin 37 top, 44, 53 top

Michael Holford 14 left, 18 right, 35 top
Hulton Picture Company 21 bottom, 30, 37 bottom,
    45 bottom
Hutchison Library 31 top, 41 bottom, 43
MacDonald/Aldus Archive 39, 42, 45 top
Magnum 32
Mansell Collection 33, 40, 50 left
Marion and Tony Morrison 34, 35 bottom, 36, 38
National Maritime Museum 14 right
Oxford Scientific Films 13 bottom, 19, 31 bottom
Photo Library of Australia 49 top
Popperfoto 47 bottom
Rapho 5
Ronan Picture Library 18 left
Science Photo Library 58
Frank Spooner Pictures 59 centre
Charles Swithinbank 55 top
Viking Museum, Oslo 10

Maps by: Lovell Johns Ltd
Illustrated by: Nick Shewring (Garden Studios),
Eugene Fleury

Series editor: Neil Champion
Educational consultant: Dr Alistair Ross
Designed by: Groom and Pickerill
Picture research: Ann Usborne

Contents

Words found in **bold** are explained
in the glossary on pages 60 and 61

1: REASONS TO EXPLORE

The Earliest Explorers

This map shows the major routes of migration taken by early people (100,000 to 10,000 years ago). As you can see, they spread out from what is today the African and South-east Asian tropics. ▶

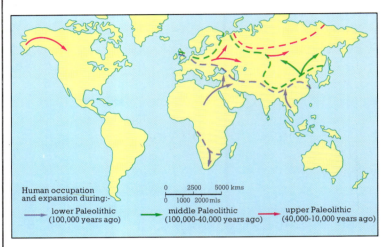

Human occupation and expansion during:-

lower Paleolithic (100,000 years ago)

middle Paleolithic (100,000-40,000 years ago)

upper Paleolithic (40,000-10,000 years ago)

▲ A community of Stone Age people, at around the end of the last ice age (10,000 years ago). You can see on the cave wall pictures drawn of the animals they hunted.

What is Exploration?

The urge to explore has been in the human race ever since our ancestors evolved in the tropics over a million years ago. But only quite recently – in the last 2,000 years – have we been able to explore far from home. Over the course of half a million years, humans migrated from the **tropics** of Africa and South-east Asia to the harsher lands of Europe and China. By the end of the last **ice age** (11,000 years ago) humans had spread to every continent except Antarctica. So it is wrong to think of explorers 'discovering' unknown places. Most places have been found and lived in by someone, at some time.

But those early humans were not strictly speaking explorers. They moved from place to place looking for good places to live, not necessarily to explore. Explorers are different. There are many reasons to explore – to find places to settle, to trade, to steal, to learn, to become famous, to spread a religion. But there is one thing all explorers have in common. They keep some contact with home. They want to bring or send knowledge of the world back to their homelands.

Expanding Nations

Often, exploring was done by people from countries that were rapidly developing: countries with people wanting to know what was beyond the horizon, traders who wanted precious metals, spices or gems, military commanders who wanted to find useful bases on other lands and scholars who wanted knowledge of other people and their ideas and inventions.

These are powerful motives. They had to be, to persuade men and women to undertake journeys of incredible hardship and which were very expensive. There have not been many countries or many centuries that could support these explorers. But many great civilizations, from the past up to the present day, have used time and resources in exploration and individuals of great courage have risen to meet the challenges.

▲ These paintings of bison are on the walls of caves in Lascaux, southern France. The paintings were done about 30,000 years ago by people known as Cro-Magnon, after the place where their remains were first found. Following their prey, Cro-Magnon people became Europe's first explorers.

These peoples had lived in their traditional tribal manner for hundreds and maybe thousands of years before they were 'discovered' by white Europeans. ▼

New Zealand Maori

Amazonian Indian

Australian aborigine

Inuit (Eskimo)

North American Indian

5

2: THE ANCIENT WORLD

The Birth of Exploration

Once, most Mediterranean shores were clean and green like this. ▼

The Mediterranean Sea is a perfect training ground for sailors. It is 4,000 km (2,500 miles) long but the waters are relatively calm, warm and clear, with many islands that provide secure harbours for ships.

Until about 300 BC, no one living there had any idea what lay beyond its shores. Westwards through the Straits of Gibraltar was the ocean, empty of land as far as anyone knew. The same ocean was believed to be part of a huge river encircling Europe and Africa – the World, to the people living there. Eastwards, the Caspian Sea and the Persian Gulf were thought to be part of the same great river.

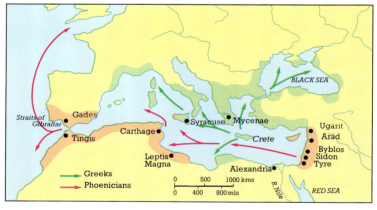

BLACK SEA

Straits of Gibraltar · Gades · Tingis · Carthage · Syracuse · Mycenae · Crete · Leptis Magna · Alexandria · Ugarit · Arad · Byblos · Sidon · Tyre · R. Nile · RED SEA

→ Greeks
→ Phoenicians

0   500   1000 kms
0   400   800 mls

Carthage in Tunisia is now a ruin standing in desert. When it was founded by Phoenicians in about 800 BC, it was a port set in fertile land – an ideal base for empire-builders who were also seafarers. ▶

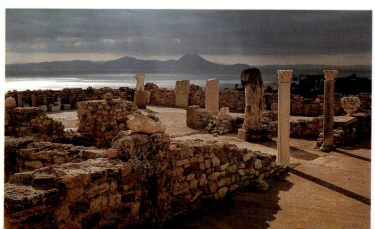

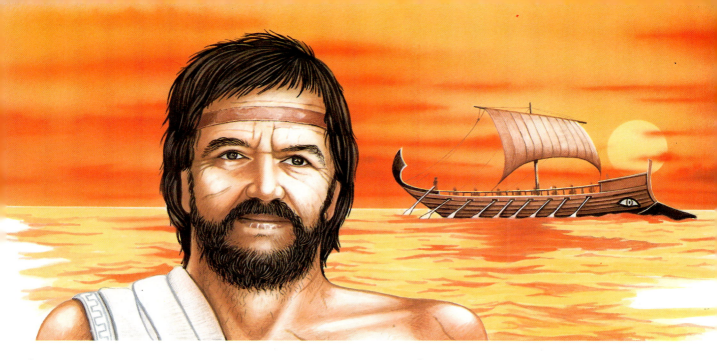

Navigation

If travellers ventured to the edge of the known world, it was almost impossible to record accurately what they saw. Sailors steered by wind direction, stars, currents and land sightings. There were no **compasses**, so if there was cloud, they could not tell accurately in which direction they were travelling. Though **geographers** knew the Earth was round, no one knew its size. There were no clocks, so time was measured in days only.

The Ancient Egyptians

The greatest of the Mediterranean's early **civilizations** – Egypt – only explored south of its lands twice – in about 2,500 BC and again 1,000 years later. The Egyptians built a canal to join the Nile to the Red Sea. They journeyed to Arabia and East Africa, an area they called Punt, where they bought rare and expensive materials like turquoise, ivory, **frankincense** and **myrrh**.

In about 600 BC, the pharoah of Egypt, Necho, started trading with Punt. But the canal that had linked the Nile to the Red Sea had silted up, and Necho paid a Phoenician fleet to explore another route around Africa. They made it; but it took three years, too long for the Egyptians to use the route for trade.

▲ An artist's impression of one of the ancient world's greatest legendary explorers: Ulysses. The journey he took from Troy (a ruined city in Turkey) to his home of Ithaca (an island off Greece) was described by the blind Greek poet, Homer, about 2,500 years ago.

Did You Know?

Hanno, a Phoenician from Carthage, set out with 60 ships to set up colonies on the west coast of Africa. Then he went further, right round the bulge of West Africa. On his way, he saw crocodiles and hippopotamuses, a volcano and 'women with hairy bodies', probably chimpanzees. 'We secured three women, who bit and scratched', he wrote. 'But we killed and flayed them, and brought the hides to Carthage.'

The Greeks

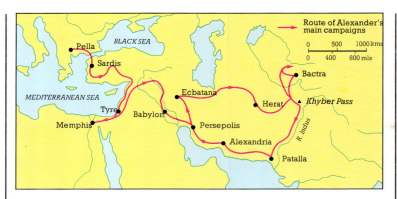

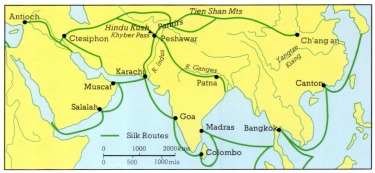

(*Top*) A map showing the route Alexander the Great took when he set out to conquer the known world, in 334 BC.
(*Bottom*) A map showing the ancient silk route, going from South-west Asia to China. ▶

The head of Alexander the Great copied from an ancient coin. He was one of the greatest travellers of the ancient world. ▼

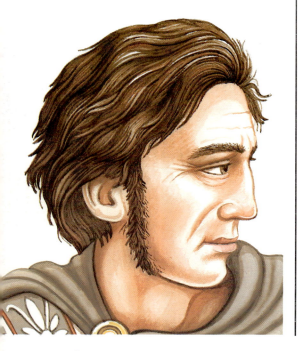

The Greeks were the greatest explorers of the ancient world, setting up over 100 colonies all around the Mediterranean and the Black Sea. Then – about 400 BC – they looked outwards.

Alexander the Great

In 334 BC, Alexander, the 23-year-old king of Macedonia (at that time, not yet part of Greece) led his army eastwards in a massive **campaign** to conquer Persia (now Iran) and India. He dreamed of conquering the whole world, before he found out it was bigger than he thought. He reached Afghanistan, marched through the Khyber Pass and continued down the Indus. The route back led through present-day Iraq and Turkey.

This astonishing 10 year journey, in which tens of thousands of people covered 32,000 km (20,000 miles), gave the Greeks accurate information of the lands between the Mediterranean and India. But Alexander died in Babylon, near present-day Baghdad, at the age of 33.

Exploring the North

Very few people had headed into the damp, cold lands of northern Europe. One of the first to do so, a few years after Alexander's death, was a Greek named Pytheas. He was a geographer from Massalia (present-day Marseilles). Like all true explorers, he was after knowledge: he wanted to find out whether Britain was an island or not.

Having discovered it was, he went on to a land he called Thule, where he said 'there is neither sea nor air, but a mixture like sea-lung'. By 'sea-lung', he might have meant an arctic fog. What did he see? Iceland? The Shetlands? Norway? No one knows, and the name Thule came to stand for some legendary place lying far to the north of the known world.

The Romans were a practical people eager to trade and make money. They probed the rich lands to the south and east. In AD 14-37, a merchant, Hippalus, used the monsoon winds to sail from Arabia round to India. A few years later the Emperor Nero sent an expedition to try to discover the source of the Nile. They reached the Sudd, vast swamps of rotting vegetation which give Sudan its name and which no other European was to see for 1,800 years.

The Silk Road

The Europeans of the Mediterranean were not the only great explorers of the ancient world. Far to the east, in China, people had a particular reason to make links westwards – they wanted to export **silk**, much prized by the rich in Europe. No one in the west knew how silk was made (it comes from the larvae of the silk-moth feeding on mulberry trees). The trade-routes to the west were opened by a Chinese explorer, Chang Chi'en, who between 138 and 126 BC explored the Tien Shan, Pamirs and Hindu Kush as far west as the Khyber Pass.

In the late fourth century, a Chinese Buddhist monk, Fa-Hsien, set out to explore the origins of his religion. It took him 15 years to wander across the Himalayas to India as far south as Sri Lanka.

Part of the Silk Road in Kirgizia, southern Russia. ▼

3: EXPANDING NATIONS

The Vikings

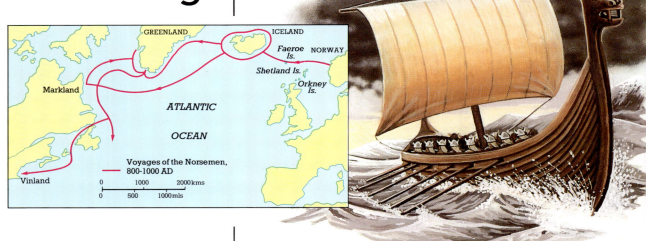

GREENLAND

ICELAND

Faeroe Is.   NORWAY

Shetland Is.

Orkney Is.

Markland

ATLANTIC

OCEAN

Voyages of the Norsemen, 800-1000 AD

0   1000   2000 kms

0   500   1000 mls

Vinland

▲ The Vikings travelled from Scandinavia to 'Vinland' (see map above) in open long boats, like the one above and below. ▼

More than 1,000 years ago, another great nation of explorers arose: the Vikings. They were great sailors, used to the steep, indented shores of Scandinavia. In the ninth century they undertook a series of explorations. They first went south and east, hauling their ships from river to river, right across Russia to Constantinople (now Istanbul) which they reached in AD 860.

Sailing Westwards
At the same time, other Vikings sailed westwards, in sturdy ships called knorrs. The knorrs were big enough to take 20 to 30 people, with cattle and food. The only shelter from the icy winds and driving rains was **smocks** and leather sleeping bags.

Island-hopping from the Orkneys and the Shetlands, the Vikings reached Iceland in AD 860. Some, driven off course by storms, reported seeing another land far to the west.

St Brendan in his currach

For a century, no one followed up the reports. Then in AD 982, Eric the Red, named after his red hair and beard, was banished from Iceland for three years for **manslaughter**. He set off to explore the land his ancestors had seen years before and returned with news of the new country, which he called Greenland.

He was successful: 350 settlers went with him to establish a new colony. The climate was warmer then than it is now, and the sea, which was clear of ice, was rich in fish and birds. For 200 years, the Vikings lived well there. But after 1500, the climate became worse, and the colony slowly died out.

Discovering Vinland

The Vikings made a great discovery even further west – the land we now call America. Viking sagas tell how an Icelander, Bjarni, was blown off course to a warm, wooded land – clearly not part of treeless Greenland. Then in about AD 1000, Eric's son, a tall man known as Leif the Lucky, sailed west to Bjarni's land. He and his men spent the winter there. Leif called the place Vinland. It was an attractive place, and two other expeditions followed. Attacks by native Indians and a shortage of food made it impossible to settle.

St Brendan, the Explorer-saint

The first person ever to cross the Atlantic may have been the Irish **missionary**, St Brendan. Christianity was brought to Ireland in AD 432 by St Patrick. After that, Ireland's holy men sought out remote islands where they could live simple lives as monks. They travelled in open, hide-covered boats called **currachs**. One of these monks was St Brendan.

A book of his journey tells how, in the middle of the 6th century, he voyaged westwards to wonderful islands. The book is a great adventure story. No one knows for sure how true it is, but a modern explorer, Tim Severin, actually made the journey to America in a currach. He proved that the voyage could be made in such a boat.

If the story is true, Brendan may have gone north first, because he saw 'hard, silver, crystal columns' (icebergs, perhaps in the cold Arctic waters). Then he passed an island that was a 'globe of fire' (perhaps a volcanic eruption in Iceland), and landed in the 'promised land of the saints', which might be America or an island like those in the Bahamas.

◄ A Viking family. They were great explorers, travelling huge distances in their long boats in the summer months. They often spent the winter in Norway with their families.

Exploring the East

For centuries, the peoples of the Far East and those of Europe had traded. In the 13th century most of Asia and much of Europe was attacked by Mongols, superb horsemen from the arid, chilly plains of Central Asia, who threatened to take over all Europe and the Middle East. In the end, the death of their emperor (the great Genghis Khan) made the Mongols withdraw. Reassured, Europeans began to venture eastwards.

John Carpini
Among the first adventurers were friars, sent by the Pope and other rulers to attempt to get the Mongols to agree never to attack again. In 1245 a 60-year-old Italian friar, John Carpini, became the first westerner to travel the 4,800 km (3,000 miles) to the Mongol capital of Karakorum.

Soon afterwards, two other friars made the same year-long journey. The second, William of Rubruck, was amazed by the huge round tents, or **yurts**, the Mongols lived in, and by the way the men shaved a square bald patch on top of their heads.

Marco Polo
The friars were followed by **merchants**, the best known being Marco Polo, one of the greatest travellers of the Middle Ages. His father and uncle, Nicolo and Maffeo, made one journey to the east that lasted fifteen years. They then set out on a second, taking young Marco, aged 17.

The Arab Explorers

Like Europeans, Arabs were eager to know what the world was like beyond their frontiers. Some Arabs journeyed east to China by land and sea; some went north and met Vikings and Russians; in the 12th century, one came to Denmark and England.

The greatest of all Arab travellers was Ibn Battuta, a Moroccan who in 1325 left home alone at the age of 22 to visit the holy cities of Mecca and Medina. He went on to travel 75,000 miles through North and East Africa, the Middle East, southern Russia, India, China and Southeast Asia. He even gives a description of the gigantic mythical bird the **roc**, famous from the stories of Sinbad the Sailor (probably what he saw was not a bird at all, but a mirage of a distant island).

When he finally arrived home he was 45. He spent the next 30 years until his death writing about his adventures.

A map showing the travels of Ibn Battuta, the famous Arab explorer of the 14th century. ▶

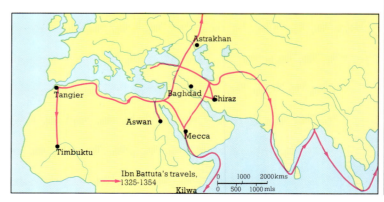

Ibn Battuta's travels, 1325-1354

Astrakhan
Tangier
Baghdad
Shiraz
Aswan
Mecca
Timbuktu
Kilwa

0 1000 2000kms
0 500 1000 mls

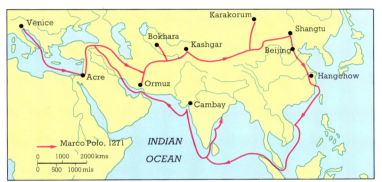

▲ The Great Wall of China, mainly built around 300 BC to keep out war-like nomads, astonished the first visitors from Europe.

◄ A map showing the journey made by Marco Polo from Venice to Khanbalik (Beijing) and back. The journey took 21 years in all.

In 1275, he and his uncle and father arrived at the court of the **Great Khan**, Kublai, in Khanbalik (modern Beijing). They were astonished by the Khan's palace, with its gold and silver walls and hall that could seat 6,000 people. The Khan employed Marco to travel round the Chinese empire and write down what he saw. He saw many things to amaze him. The Khan was given 100,000 horses on his birthday, Marco notes with awe. He saw the great city of Kinsai (now Hangchow) with its 12,000 bridges; and huge ocean-going **junks** with sixty cabins. He went on to travel round other parts of Asia – India, Sri Lanka, Myanma and Indonesia. He wrote about his travels when he returned home in 1295.

For 50 years after Marco Polo, merchants, scholars and missionaries went east, until the region between Europe and China was taken over by **Muslim** nations, hostile to the Christian West.

▲ There are four eggs in this picture. The egg of the extinct elephant bird (left) is massive compared to that of an ostrich (centre left), chicken (centre right) and a tiny hummingbird (right). Legend claims that the parent bird, known as the roc, was big enough to carry off humans.

Around Africa

The Europeans, Arabs and Chinese all lived in roughly the same climate. Other regions were, they thought, impossible to live in. To the north lay wastes of ice and snow; to the south they thought was a hellish place of fire, where the Sun boiled the waters. No one knew about the Phoenicians' journey round Africa many hundreds of years before.

Henry the Navigator

The Portuguese were the first Europeans to start sailing south along the coast of Africa. One of the king's sons, Henry the Navigator, who lived about 500 years ago, was keenly interested in exploration and voyages. In the 1440s, he sent out many explorers. In 1474, the explorers crossed the **Equator** for the first time, though many died from fever and **malaria**.

Legends spoke of a great Christian empire ruled by a king called Prester John further to

A 17th-century map of Africa shows the coast-line accurately to India. But the interior was unknown – the Nile is wrongly shown connecting with the Congo (now the Zaire). ▶

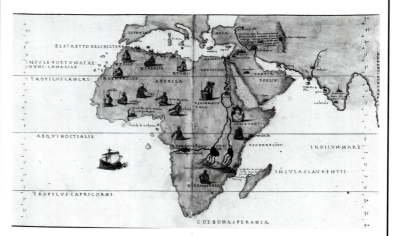

▲ Prince Henry the Navigator of Portugal, a grim, scholarly man, was so named because he financed so many voyages. He himself never went on any.

the south. These tales, combined with the desire to find a way around Africa to India, inspired a later Portuguese king, John II, to send two men, Pedro da Covilhao and Bartholomew Dias, to explore.

Covilhao started from the Red Sea, and went eastwards to India. He then turned inland, towards Ethiopia, in search of Prester John. What he found was a country that had had its own kind of Christianity for centuries. He settled there until his death, 30 years later.

Meanwhile, in 1487, Dias and his crew had gone south past West Africa and been driven by storms so far from the southern tip of Africa they did not see its cliffs and peaks until they returned in 1488. They named it the Cape of Storms. It was renamed the Cape of Good Hope by Prince John when he heard their news and realized that his ships could now sail east to India to trade.

To India by Sea

This was done years later by Vasco da Gama. It was a difficult journey. He returned from India across the Indian Ocean, sailing into head-winds. It took four months, and 30 of the crew died of **scurvy**. He had been away two years and had opened up a sea route to the East. Now precious spices could be brought to Europe without entering hostile countries.

▲ Sir Mortimer Wheeler (left), one of the first archaeologists to excavate the island site of Kilwa, off the East African coast. Many Chinese objects of the 12th to 14th centuries were discovered here.

The ruins of a palace on the island of Kilwa. Kilwa was at the centre of the trading that took place along the East African coast. ▼

Columbus and the New World

Christopher Columbus was always determined to be rich and famous as a great explorer. He knew nothing of the Viking voyages to America, but he knew the Earth was round and believed it would be possible – and quicker – to sail west to Asia rather than around East Africa. He was misled by the maps of the day and Marco Polo's writings. He thought that by travelling west over the Atlantic Ocean he would come to the Moluccas.

In 1492, he got his chance. Born in Italy, he had settled in Portugal; but it was the Spanish king and queen, Ferdinand and Isabella, who backed his expedition. They saw financial benefits coming to them if a quicker route to the East Indies was found. With three small ships and 100 men, he sailed westwards into the unknown.

The Bahamas

Two months later, just when the crew were ready to **mutiny**, they sighted an island. On the shore stood some people, who swam out to the ships to trade parrots and spears for

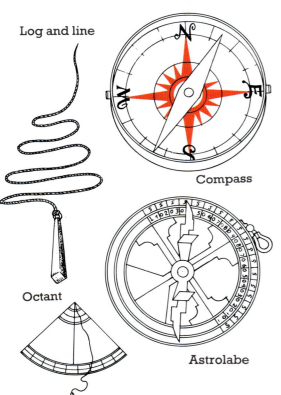

Log and line

Compass

Octant

Astrolabe

▲ Instruments commonly used to navigate across open seas.

This is a cut-away illustration of Columbus' first ship, the *Santa Maria*. You can see how the sailors on board would have lived on long voyages. Conditions were cramped and tough. ▶

clothing and beads. The island was in the Bahamas. Columbus had no idea where he was. He thought it was part of India. So he called the natives, 'Indians'. The islands he discovered are called the West Indies. He arrived back in Spain only five months after setting out – a surprisingly easy trip.

Columbus returned full of promises that gold and slaves would make other trips pay well. Within months, he was off again, with 14 ships and 1,200 men, to settle a large island he had called Hispaniola (now two countries, Haiti and the Dominican Republic). But there was little food, no gold, and the people already living there were hostile.

In 1502, after a third trip exploring the coastline of what is now Venezuela, Columbus was sent out on his last voyage. He was still eager to find Asia by travelling west. This time, he landed on the coast of Central America, naming it Costa Rica. By now he was in his 50s, and ill. He died in 1506, still not knowing that he had began to open up a whole new continent.

▲ After two months at sea, the sight of a West Indian island like this must have cheered Columbus's exhausted sailors.

The Man Who Named a Continent

Amerigo Vespucci worked for the great Italian family, the Medicis, who sent him to Spain in 1491 to work in a business selling supplies to ships. Here he met Columbus. Between 1497 and 1504 he himself went on several voyages across the Atlantic. No one is sure how many journeys he made, because new discoveries were valuable, and he kept the details secret. What is certain is that he sailed along the coast of South America, past the mouth of the Amazon. At first, like Columbus, he thought he was exploring part of Asia. But as he went further south, it was clear that the land he saw was not Asia. In 1507 – a year after Columbus's death – a geographer called Martin Waldseemueller suggested that since Amerigo found this new world, it should be named 'Amerige or America'. The name stuck.

Around the World

A map showing the routes of Ferdinand Magellan and del Cano (the man who took over command after Magellan was killed in the Philippines). ▶

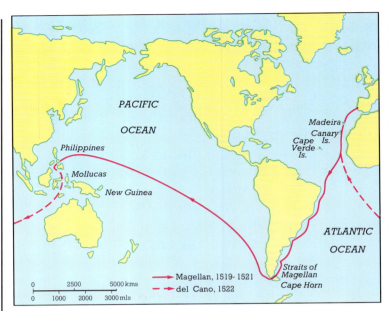

▲ In this portrait, Ferdinand Magellan is shown as a calm, scholarly man. But he was also a brutal, tough sea-dog who drove his men ruthlessly.

A 16th-century Portuguese map of South America (*right*) shows the Straits of Magellan. The land southwards was thought to be part of another continent. But sailors at least knew they could reach the Pacific through the Straits (far right), if the weather was good. ▶

After Columbus and Vespucci's voyages, the Spaniards could believe there really was a way to the East by travelling west. Ferdinand Magellan was Portuguese but he worked for the Spanish. He promised to find a way round the southern tip of South America.

In September 1519 he set off. He had five ships and a crew of 237. They had huge amounts of trade goods. From the start, it was a hard journey. Near the tip of South America, Magellan had to quell a mutiny by executing one of his captains. One ship was wrecked in a storm.

The Strait of Magellan

Magellan was aiming for one of the most tempestuous regions on earth, with mountainous seas and icy winds. Magellan found a way to avoid the Cape – through a narrow twisting channel, now named the Strait of Magellan. So frightened were some of his men that one of the remaining ships gave up and turned back.

Into the Pacific

Magellan emerged into the Pacific with three ships. He continued westward for three months. Food and water dwindled. The men had to survive on rotten biscuits, rats and leather. Twenty men died of scurvy.

In March 1521, they arrived at what we call today the Philippines. Magellan set about converting the local people to Christianity. On one island, the people resisted and killed 40 of the Europeans including Magellan.

With only half the crew-members still alive, one of the ships was abandoned. The *Trinidad* and *Vittorio* finally reached the Moluccas in January 1522 and took on huge cargoes of spices. After repairs, the *Trinidad* headed back across the Pacific, only to be captured by Portuguese. The *Vittorio* limped home nine months later. The surviving crew, just 18 of them, were the first people to sail round the world.

The Dragon Who Circled the World

The second great explorer to sail around the world was one of England's greatest adventurers, Sir Francis Drake. He was in the service of Queen Elizabeth I, employed to raid Spanish ships bringing treasure from South America. On one raid, in 1569, he saw the Pacific over the thin neck of land that is now Panama. He called upon God to allow him 'to sail once in an English ship upon that sea.'

In 1577, he got his chance. The Queen asked him to find the great Southern Continent, Terra Australis, that was supposed to exist in the South Pacific. He could then sail on to the Moluccas for spices before turning back. And if he could plunder a few more Spanish galleons, the Queen told him, so much the better.

At the tip of South America, they were so battered by storms that one ship sank and another turned back. But the storm led to a great discovery. Driven off course, Drake found open water to the south, where the Atlantic and the Pacific joined, though he didn't see Cape Horn.

Working his way through the Strait of Magellan, Drake then crept up the west coast of South America, plundering Spaniards (including one **galleon** that was carrying 20 tons of silver). Searching for a passage back to the Atlantic, he went as far north as Canada. There was no way back eastwards, so he decided to sail round the world.

He returned after almost three years with plunder worth at today's value £1,500,000. The Spaniards called him El Draque – The Dragon.

4: OPENING THE PACIFIC

The Southern Continent

A map showing the routes of the Dutchman, Abel Tasman, and the French explorer, Bougainville. They opened up exploration of the great continent of Australasia. ▶

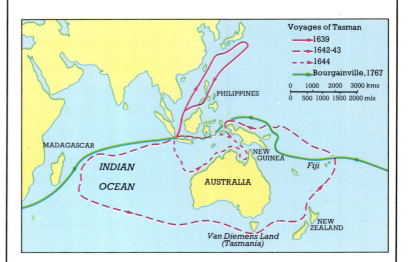

In the late 16th century, the Spaniards wanted to be the first to find the great continent that was thought to lie in the South Pacific. They even had a name for the dream continent: Australia, 'the land of the south.' No one knew then that the continent actually existed, because the Spaniards never saw it. They came close on several **expeditions**. They mapped many of the thousands of islands in the region, and one expedition, led by Luiz de Torres, followed the coast of New Guinea and saw islands off the Australian coast.

The Dutch

It was the Dutch who took the lead in Pacific exploration. One Dutch expedition, led by Willem Jantszoon, avoided the Strait of Magellan and went round the Cape. He named it Cape Horn after one of their ships. In 1606 he made the first recorded sighting of Australia. And the Dutchman, Abel Tasman, became the first to sail right round Australia in 1642. In

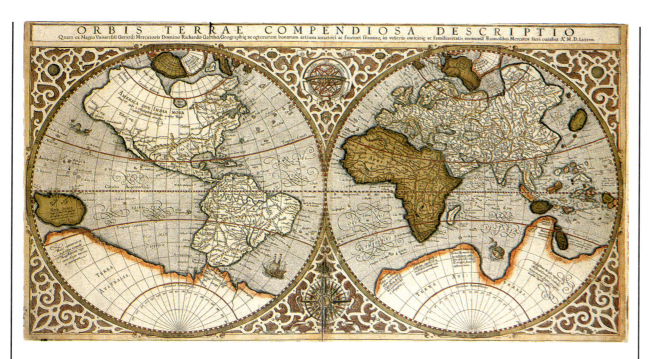

doing so, he saw the islands he named Tasmania and New Zealand.

After Tasman, people knew roughly the major land masses and oceans of the world. The task of filling in the details took another 100 years. The men who did it were mostly French and English.

Count Bougainville

The greatest of the French explorers was the Count Bougainville, who in 1767 explored the islands of the Pacific. He made many scientific discoveries. This was in part due to one of the scientists' **valets**, Jeanne Baré, who became an expert **botanist**. Baré was a woman. She was one of the first women to be part of a great voyage of exploration.

▲ This map of 1595 shows the massive southern continent – Terra Australis, 'land of the south' – that scientists thought must exist to balance the wieght of land north of the Equator. The scientists were right in a way. There were actually two 'lands of the south' to be discovered – Australia and Antarctica.

◄ When white men first came to Tasmania, they killed many of the Aborigines. Others died of drink and disease. The last ones, shown here, died in the 1850s and 1860s.

Captain Cook

A map showing the three voyages of Captain Cook across the Pacific Ocean and around what we now call Australia. ▶

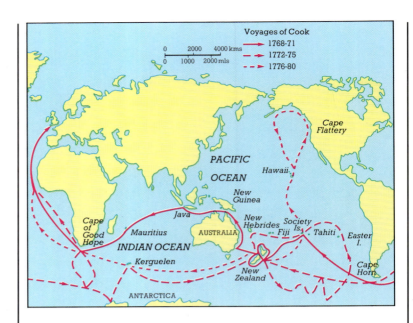

James Cook was born in 1728. He was the greatest of Pacific explorers and he filled the last great gaps on the world map. On his first voyage he planned to record the planet Venus as it moved between the Earth and the Sun. He also had a secret mission – to see if there was an undiscovered southern continent beyond Australia. Many people still argued that such a land was necessary to balance the weight of Europe and Asia in the North.

Cook was the son of an agricultural labourer. As a teenager he became a merchant seaman on coalships. But he was brilliant at mathematics, an expert navigator, and above all a great leader. He took care of his crew making sure that they keep clean and eat fresh food to avoid ill-health and disease.

Cook's Voyages

In the first of his three voyages (1768-71), Cook made the observations of Venus from Tahiti, sailed 2,400 km (1,500 miles) south (finding nothing but islands), and mapped New Zealand. On the Australian coast, he discovered Botany Bay, where British **convicts** were later sent. He went on to explore the **Great Barrier Reef**, and proved that New Guinea was not connected to Australia.

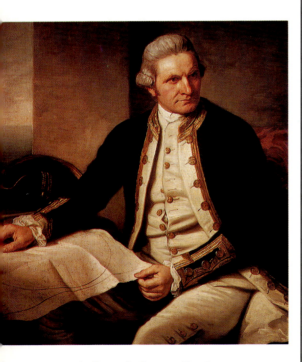

▲ Captain James Cook was both a superb sailor and a great leader. He was described by the novelist Fanny Burney as 'the most humane and gentle navigator that ever went out upon discoveries'.

◄ Captain Cook's ship, the *Endeavour*. It was a sturdy vessel, 30 m (97 ft 8 ins) long, weighing 366 tons.

His second voyage (1772-75) took him further south than anyone had ever been, into realms of icebergs and fog. 'Ropes like wires,' he wrote. 'Sails like plates of metal.' But he did not sail far enough south to discover Antarctica.

The third voyage (1776-80) was to look for a passage into the Pacific, north of Canada – the Northwest Passage sought by Elizabethan explorers. He found nothing but ice. He returned to Hawaii where tribal priests proclaimed him a god and insisted that the islanders hand over supplies by the boatload. The Hawaiians grew bitter: a fight broke out on shore, during which Cook was clubbed and stabbed to death.

◄ When Cook was driven back to Hawaii by gales, the islanders turned hostile. Cook, in a rare display of temper, shot one of the natives. The mob attacked and stabbed him to death, as the rest of the crew scrambled for the boats.

5: ACROSS THE NEW WORLD

The Northwest Passage

▲ Martin Frobisher was a strong Yorkshireman with a foul temper 'Who swore no small oaths'.

While the Spanish set about seizing Central and South America, British explorers turned their attention northwards. They were convinced that there was a way round the top of North America to the spice-rich East and the fabled land of Cathay, which we now call China.

First to try were the Cabots – John and his son Sebastian. Their reports of icy seas, smothering fog, and dead-ends turned attention to the north-east, but the wastes of northern Russia seemed equally hopeless.

Sir Martin Frobisher

First to make a serious search for the Northwest Passage was Martin Frobisher. In 1576 he passed Greenland, and found himself in what he thought was a passage westwards. In fact, he was in an inlet of Baffin Island. Soon he was surrounded by hostile **Inuit** in **kayaks**. When five of his men went off exploring and were never seen again, Frobisher captured one of the Inuit, hoping to use him as a hostage to get his men back. He returned with the Inuit, and with some glittering rocks which he said were gold. Another expedition proved him wrong: the rocks he brought back were pyrites, 'fools' gold', and utterly worthless.

The next attempt, led by John Davis, was more scientific. His three expeditions (1585-7) produced much good information, but no way through to the Pacific.

An ill-fated voyage to this icy wasteland was made by Henry Hudson, who had already explored the area around present-day New York, naming the great river after himself. In

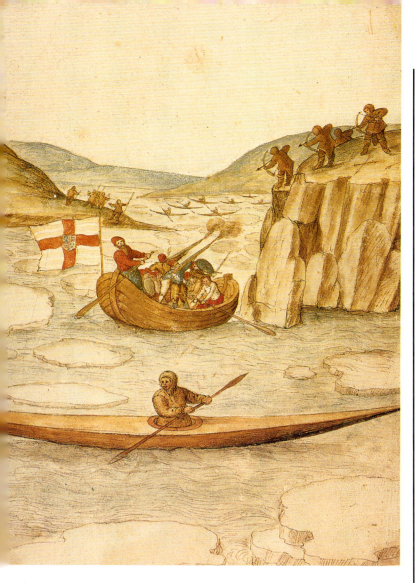

◄ Searching for the North-West Passage, Frobisher's men were attacked by Eskimos (*left*). Frobisher was so furious that he had one of the Eskimos (*below*) seized and brought home to England. ▼

For explorers, polar bears can be a menace. They can kill a man with one blow. ▼

1610, he set off to find the route to the East. After wintering in an immense bay, also named after him, the crew mutinied, and set him adrift in an open boat, leaving him and his eight companions to a miserable death.

Others who came after Hudson mapped the bay and the islands, and concluded that any further expeditions were a waste of time. But one thing had been discovered from the journeys – a way into northern Canada that avoided the area where the French were, with whom the British were fighting at this time. There is a route that leads through to Asia, but it was not discovered until 1903, when more sophisticated navigation equipment and strong ships to withstand the crushing ice were in use.

Moving Westwards

Early exploration to the north of Canada, revealed two great sources of wealth – fish and furs. It was the French who pioneered routes leading into the heart of North America, travelling in birch-bark canoes and learning to trade with the Indians, then working their way southwards, behind the young English colonies growing up on the east coast.

In 1534, Jacques Cartier became the first European to see the great bay of the St Lawrence River. The following year, he made his way up it, guided by Indians, past a pro-

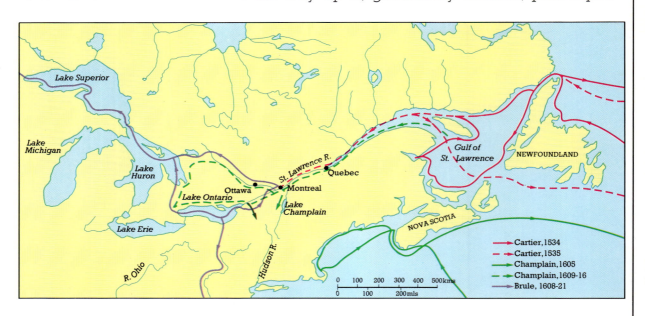

▲ A map showing the routes taken by the expeditions that moved westwards into the interior of Canada and the United States (as both these countries were eventually to be called).

montory where Quebec now stands, to a stockaded village set on heights he called Mount Royal (now Montreal).

Sixty years later, Samuel de Champlain tried to find a way right across the continent. In doing so he made friends with the Huron and Algonquin Indians in attacks on the Iroquois, who lived to the south. Champlain then returned to help administer the colony he had helped found.

It was a young **interpreter**, Etienne Brulé who extended Champlain's explorations to the Great Lakes. He reached the far end of Lake Superior, almost the centre of the continent.

Other Frenchmen followed, working their way west and south to the headwaters of the Mississippi. The river was finally explored to its mouth by Robert de la Salle in 1682, who claimed the whole Mississippi valley for France, naming it Louisiana in honour of his king, Louis XIV.

It was not until much later that anyone made the overland trek to the Pacific coast, though the British and Russians reached it by sea. Then a Scot, Alexander MacKenzie, set out westwards from the Great Slave Lake up the river now named after him. Finding that it veered northwards, he turned back, to set out again due west. He and his men eventually struggled over the Rockies, reaching the ocean after a two-month journey on July 22, 1793.

▲ Trading with the indigenous peoples, the tribal Indians, was an essential part of life for the early explorers and settlers. In exchange for guns and metal tools the white Europeans got much-prized furs and cloth.

Watched by Indians, Jacques Cartier's 1535 expedition sails westward along the St Lawrence. ▼

Breakout from the East

The life of a frontiersman was often dangerous. They traversed unknown territory, ran the risk of being killed by native Indians or attacked by wild animals, such as bears and wolves. ▶

Essential clothing for a frontiersman: the warm and hard-wearing buckskin shirt, raccoon or beaver-skin hat, musket and powder horn. ▼

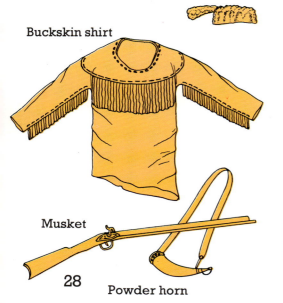

Raccoon or beaver hat

Buckskin shirt

Musket

Powder horn

28

Settlement had begun on the American coast in the 16th century. By the mid-18th century, there were so many settlers that they needed to open up new lands to the west.

Daniel Boone

For a hundred years, lone frontiersmen had crossed the Appalachian Mountains to hunt deer for their skins. The best known of these backwoodsmen was Daniel Boone, who spent years exploring and hunting in Kentucky. Within 15 years of his return in 1771, 30,000 people had followed his footsteps.

Alexander MacKenzie was the first European to cross from coast to coast. This was in 1793. His successful journey to the Pacific inspired President Jefferson to propose an official expedition. The two chosen to lead the expedition were Jefferson's secretary, Meriwether Lewis, and an acquaintance of his, William Clark. The expedition set out in 1804, travelling 2,500 km (1,600 miles) through the

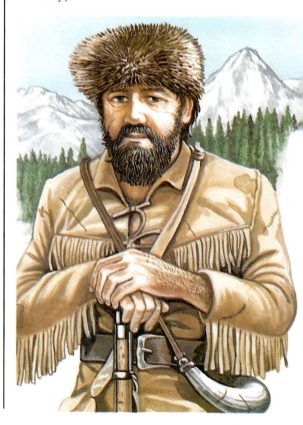

◀ Rolling along trails pioneered by the first explorers of the American West, a wagon train heads away from the mid-western plains into the Rocky Mountains.

A frontiersman, of around the time of Daniel Boone (the second half of the eighteenth century). ▼

mid-western prairies to the headwaters of the Missouri River in the Rockies.

Then they were into unknown territory, amidst mountains that seemed impassable. Fortunately one member of the expedition was married to a **Shoshoni** woman, who guided them and won over other members of the tribe, from whom the white men bought horses. After crossing many passes, they descended the Columbia River to the Pacific.

They returned safely after covering over 12,000 km (7,500 miles) in 28 months.

The South, however, was still largely un-explored by the Americans. As Lewis and Clark were returning, a 26-year-old lieu-tenant, Zebulon Pike, left to explore the headwaters of the Mississippi. On later trips, he explored the Colorado ranges that include the startlingly beautiful Pike's Peak. These areas bordered on Spanish New Mexico, and Pike's reports opened the way for trade with Mexico.

In the wake of these discoveries came the settlers, driving wagons to the west coast along the Santa Fe, Oregon and California trails. In 1845, John O'Sullivan, editor of the New York *Morning News* wrote: 'It is our manifest destiny to possess the whole of the continent.' By then, the Americans were well on their way to doing so.

6: THE WILDS OF ASIA

Across Russia

▲ A painting of Peter the Great (1672-1725). He sent out expeditions to explore the northeast territories of Russia.

Until the 1550s, Siberia was largely an unknown wasteland. But like northern Canada, it was rich in furs. In 1581, 1,600 **Cossacks** under their leader Yermak Timofeiev marched over the Ural Mountains to begin the Russian conquest of northern Asia. By 1640, Russians had reached the Pacific on the far side.

Peter the Great

Under Peter the Great (1672-1725), more explorers went northeast to find out if Russia and America meet. The man who did more than anyone to explore the area was Vitus Bering, who sailed north along the east coast of Siberia in 1728. Eventually, forcing his way through pack-ice, he found the coastline swung away to the west. He had discovered the gap between Asia and America, the 90 km (55 mile) wide strait that bears his name.

On a later voyage in 1741, he explored the coast of Alaska, returning to winter on the barren Bering Island. For shelter, his 77 men had to dig holes in the ground and cover them with sails. Twenty-eight men died of scurvy that winter, among them Bering him-

A map showing the routes Vitus Bering took exploring the vast expanse of Siberia and other parts of Russia. ▶

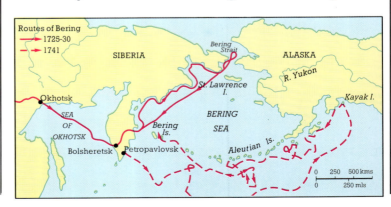

Routes of Bering
1725-30
1741

SIBERIA
Bering Strait
ALASKA
R. Yukon
St. Lawrence I.
Kayak I.
Okhotsk
SEA OF OKHOTSK
BERING SEA
Bering Is.
Bolsheretsk
Petropavlovsk
Aleutian Is.

0 250 500 kms
0 250 mls

self. As a result of his work, Alaska became Russian, and remained so until America bought it in 1867 for 7,200,000 dollars.

Exploring the Tien Shan Mountains

Further south, exploration of the unmapped Tien Shan mountains began in 1857, and in 1870, the greatest of Russian travellers, Nikolai Przhevalsky, set off on the first of five immense journeys across Mongolia, China and the mountains of Central Asia – a huge, empty area of swamp, sand and icy plateaus.

He died at Lake Issyk-Kul, high in the Tien Shan mountains in 1888, and failed to reach Lhasa, the capital of Tibet. He is still remembered for his records of plants and animals. He discovered the only known wild horse, which is named after him.

▲ The Tien Shan mountains form a massive 1,500-mile barrier between Russia and China.

▲ Przhevalski's horse is a stocky, woolly species well adapted to the icy Central Asian winters.

31

The Himalayas

▲ Rock-climbing and mountaineering became popular serious sports in the nineteenth century. But it wasn't until the 20th century that the world's highest peak, Mount Everest, was conquered.

The Potala is the fortress-palace of the Dalai Lama, the Tibetan ruler. It overlooks Lhasa, once so inaccessible to Europeans it was called The Forbidden City. ▶

After the Polos, few westerners ever ventured over the Himalayas to China. A Spaniard, Benedict de Goes, did so in 1603-5, aiming to make contact with any Chinese Christians. Then in 1661, two **Jesuit** missionaries – a German, John Grueber, and a Belgian, Albert d'Orville – set out to establish a regular European trade route from China to India. They became the first Europeans ever to see Lhasa, the capital of Tibet.

◀ The triangular peak of Everest is the highest in the world (*left*), but it is almost equalled by other Himalayan giants like Nuptse (*centre*) and Lhotse (*right*).

The Jesuits again appeared in Tibet in 1715, when an Italian, Ippolito Desideri, arrived at Lhasa. After that, Tibet fell under the influence of China, and few Europeans were able to visit Lhasa.

Map-making

Travellers and explorers usually went through the mountains by established paths. But detailed knowledge could only come from maps. The greatest of the map-makers was George Everest. He retired in 1843, but after the survey of the highest peaks was completed in 1862, the world's highest mountain was named after him.

The detailed surveying work was done by 'Learned Experts' or Pundits, many of whom were Indians. Often, to explore remote areas, they would travel in disguise as **pilgrims**, with prayer wheels and books specially made to conceal their notes. They carried strings of beads which they used to count their paces – one pundit even kept a tally of his horse's footsteps for 370 km (230 miles).

Perhaps the greatest of all Central Asian explorers was Sven Hedin. By his time, there was little original exploration left to do, but he crossed the region more times than anyone else between 1890 and the First World War. On one journey in 1894-7, he covered 19,000 km (12,000 miles) and made 552 pages of maps.

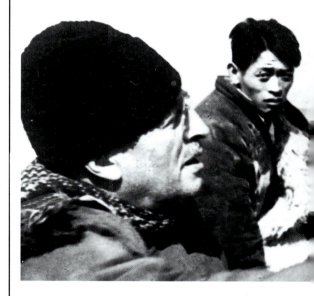

▲ Sven Hedin, the Swedish explorer, spent his whole life travelling. In this picture, taken in China when he was 70, he was leading an expedition along the Silk Road.

The Sands of Arabia

Mecca, where Mohammed (the founder of Islam) was born, is the holiest Muslim city. At the centre is the Kaaba, a square building which Muslim tradition claims was built by Abraham. Mecca is closed to non-Muslims. ▶

The heart of the Arab world, the arid area beyond the Red Sea, was a closed book to Europeans until this century. The Arabs themselves knew the geography of their own land, but their knowledge was not available to the world outside. Europeans had to discover it for themselves.

Mecca

It was not the harshness of the country but the suspicion of outsiders that kept travellers away. Indeed the holy city of **Mecca** was forbidden to non-Moslem foreigners. The only answer was disguise, an ability to speak Arabic, and a knowledge of Moslem ways.

An Italian, Ludovico di Varthema, sneaked into Mecca in about 1500. Joseph Pitts, an Englishman, was captured by pirates in 1678, sold into slavery, became a Moslem, and journeyed with his master until he escaped. The first official exploration of Arabia was made by six Danish scientists in 1762. They were unlucky: all but one died of disease.

More successful was the Swiss, Johann Burck-
hardt, who studied Arabic and worked his way
in disguise up the Nile, where in 1813 he redis-
covered the great rock temple of Abu Simbel
with its 18 m (60 feet) carvings. So respected
did he become that he was declared a Moslem
and allowed to visit Mecca.

Through the 19th century, other adventurers, most of them expert in Arabic,
gathered information about the deserts.
One such explorer was Richard Burton, who
was later to explore the Nile. After learning
Arabic he crossed Arabia disguised as a poor
Afghan.

In the First World War, the Arabs revolted
against their Turkish masters. The uprising
drew T. E. Lawrence – Lawrence of Arabia –
to explore the desert region known as the
Hejaz.

The Empty Quarter

By the 1930s, the only unexplored area was the
Empty Quarter, which was first crossed by an
outsider – Bertram Thomas – in 1930-1. He was
followed by Harry St John Philby and Wilfrid
Thesiger, who crossed the area in 1946-7.
These three men went to experience a different way of life. They lived comparatively
simply, which allowed them to develop a
complex relationship with the desert and its
inhabitants.

▲ The Empty Quarter (*top*) of
southern Arabia is the world's
largest sand desert. It is
roamed by Bedouin, who know
its scattered water-holes, but it
was first crossed by British
explorers. The last was Wilfrid
Thesiger (*above*) in 1948-50.

7: SOUTH AMERICA

The Search for El Dorado

The jungle through which the River Amazon flows is the world's largest rainforest. The river's 1,000 major tributaries contain one-third of the world's fresh water. ▼

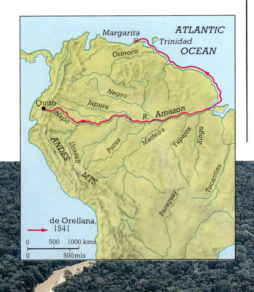

Margarita
Trinidad
ATLANTIC
OCEAN
Orinoco
Negro
Japura
Quito
Napo
R. Amazon
ANDES
Ucayali
Purus
Madeira
Tapajos
Xingu
MTS.
Paraguay
Tocantins

de Orellana,
1541

0   500   1000 kms
0   500 mls

After Columbus's discovery of America, the Spanish went into South America with one aim in mind: to get as much gold as possible. Exploration was of little interest. For over a century they seized gold and silver from the Mayas and Aztecs of Mexico and the Incas of the high Andes.

The Gilded Man

In South America, they were lured by the belief that somewhere there lay a land of gold. The myth arose because an Indian tribe in Colombia had a dramatic ceremony: every year the chief was smeared with gold dust, which he then washed off in a lake. The Spanish called the chief El Dorado, 'the gilded man'. The tribe was small and the amount of gold-dust they used was tiny, but the Spaniards came to believe that the chief was a rich king.

After the conquest of the Incas in 1533, the Spanish ruler, Francisco Pizarro, sent his brother Gonzalo off to search for El Dorado in the jungle of Ecuador. With his second-in-command, Francisco de Orellana, Gonzalo marched 80 men down from the Andes into the tropical rainforest of the Amazon basin.

Arriving at the Napo, a branch of the Amazon, they built a boat and began to explore downriver, with some men sailing and the rest struggling along the bank. After a month, they found no food but 'frogs and serpents'. Pizarro sent Orellana and 50 men ahead to look for supplies. He and his men were carried away by the current, leaving Pizarro to make his way back to the Andes.

Orellana, almost by mistake, then completed one of the greatest journeys of exploration by sailing almost 5,000 km (3,000 miles) down the Amazon to the Atlantic, becoming the first Spaniard to cross the continent.

Naming the Amazon

On the way he had numerous encounters with hostile Indians. At one point, they saw women fighting. Recalling the Greek legend of a tribe of warrior-women known as **Amazons**, Orellana named the whole area after them.

▲ Most Indian cultures in South America made gold objects, like this death mask made in Peru in about 1200 (*above*). The Spaniards stole gold in huge quantities, and were always eager to explore for more. They believed there was somewhere a fabulous city of gold because they heard that at Lake Guatavita in Colombia (*below*) a chief used to wash gold from his body. In fact, the amount of gold-dust used was minute, and no one has found any treasure in the lake. ▼

Into the Amazon

The highest mountain in South America is 6,250 m (20,500 ft). It is Chimborazo, in Ecuador. ▼

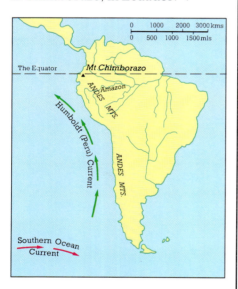

Chimborazo, one of the many snow-capped volcanoes in the Andes, was first climbed by Alexander von Humboldt. ▶

The exploration of the **Amazon basin** was mainly carried out by scientists. First into the area, in 1743, was a Frenchman, Charles-Marie de la Condamine. His main task had been to take measurements of the Earth at the Equator. But having done that high in the Andes, he descended into the Amazon, journeying to the central town of Manaus and up the Rio Negro. His reports showed the huge wealth of botanical and **zoological** research to be done.

Alexander von Humboldt

The greatest of the scientist-explorers was a young German, Alexander von Humboldt. He and his French colleague Aimé Bonpland set out in 1799, heading south from Venezuela to the Orinoco River. They recorded their experiences with the region's strange creatures – electric eels, piranhas, stingrays and freshwater dolphins. They also saw for themselves the strange Casiquiare Canal, a natural waterway that connects the Orinoco to the Amazon. On their return, they discovered one of the difficulties of research in the tropics – a third of their 12,000 plant specimens were destroyed by **humidity**.

The next stage of their journey began in the Andes, where they set out to climb the 6,250 m (20,500 foot) high volcano, Chimborazo, then thought to be the highest mountain in the world. He was within 300 m (1,000 feet) of the

summit when an impassable ravine combined with altitude sickness made him turn back. The peak was finally climbed by an Englishman, Edward Whymper, in 1880.

The Humboldt Current

Moving on south, he was puzzled by the desert conditions in Peru. He also discovered the explanation: although almost on the Equator, the sea-water was extremely cold, being swept up from the Antarctic by the current that now bears his name. This prevented rain from falling in certain areas. Also, the high Andes Mountains influenced where the rain fell.

Though he was proudest of his ascent of Chimborazo, his scientific work provided the first detailed record of the plant and animal life of South America. He was curious about everything he saw. He was called 'the greatest scientific traveller who ever lived' by another scientific explorer, Charles Darwin.

▲ The explorer-scientist Humboldt (*standing, and in close-up below*) records his findings with his colleague, Aimé Bonpland, at a campsite high in the Andes. ▼

SOUTH AMERICA

The Naturalists

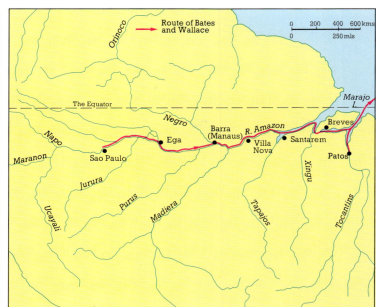

Route of Bates and Wallace

▲ While seizing a toucan for his zoological collection, Henry Bates is beset by a flock of protesting birds. Bates's book *The Naturalist on the River Amazon* remains a classic of exploration and discovery.

In the early 19th century, a number of European expeditions followed in Humboldt's footsteps.

In 1848, two Englishmen, Henry Bates and Alfred Wallace, did particularly important work, hoping to explain how different **species** arose.

Collecting Species

Bates spent over seven years in the Amazon, collecting some 14,000 species of insects, over half of them previously unknown.

Wallace's collection was largely lost in a fire on board his ship, but he went on to Malaya, where he helped work out the theory of evolution later developed by Charles Darwin.

Towards the end of the century more and more explorers came to the Amazon. An American surgeon, Hamilton Rice, tried to find the source of the Orinoco, but was driven off by hostile tribes. A Brazilian military engineer, Candido Rondon, made many hazardous journeys to meet Indian tribes in the southern Amazon. For one expedition he teamed up with the former American President Theodore Roosevelt, whose dramatic stories gave people the idea that all of the Amazon was a 'green hell'.

▲ Wildlife of the Amazon tropical rainforests.

Mapping the Amazon

Perhaps the most famous Amazon explorer was Percy Fawcett. For many years, he helped to map frontier areas, where he heard fascinating rumours of lost cities.

In 1925 he set out with his son Jack to explore the Mato Grosso. The whole expedition vanished without trace. Almost certainly they were killed by Indians, but so much publicity surrounded his strange quest that for years it was thought they might be still alive.

Though the Amazon has been mapped now, its thousands of tributaries still hold mysteries. There are still many plant and animal species to be discovered, and almost certainly Indian groups that have never seen white people.

Colonel Percy Fawcett vanished in the Amazon in 1925 searching for a lost city. No one knows what happened to him. ▼

8: INTO AFRICA

Across the Sahara

Timbuktu

In 1824, Major Alexander Laing set out to find Timbuktu. It took him over a year, during which he was almost killed by Tuareg tribesmen, but he became the first European to cross the Sahara from north to south and enter Timbuktu. He never lived to describe it – he was murdered by Tuareg soon after his arrival.

The first man to describe the city was a Frenchman, Rene Caillié, who reached it in 1828. He found it a disappointing place of mud-built houses. Once the rich crossroads of north Africa, its gold fields were now exhausted.

The mouth of the Niger was finally discovered by Richard and John Lander in 1830. The river would be a highway into the interior. The Sahara route could be abandoned.

North African traders cross the desert. ▶

Mungo Park mapped the R. Niger. ▼

At the end of the 18th century, the interior of Africa was still virtually unknown to the world outside. As with most remote places, it was known by those who lived there. It had been penetrated by earlier travellers, especially Arabs, like Ibn Battuta. But it was largely un-mapped and unrecorded. British explorers decided to change things. In 1788, under Sir Joseph Banks, who had been Cook's botanist, several of them formed an Association for Promoting the Discovery of the Interior Parts of Africa. They had several motives: scientific interest, trade, new lands to rule, and rivalry with other European countries.

The first mystery to be solved was the whereabouts of the city of Timbuktu, described 400 years earlier by Ibn Battuta.

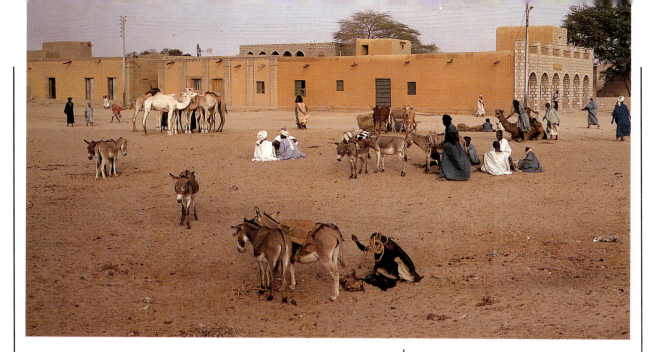

Another was the course of the great West African river, the Niger. Not even knowing which way it flowed, some thought it might somehow join up with the Nile.

▲ Timbuktu on the southern edge of the Sahara was for centuries a terminus for those crossing the desert. Here, Arabs and Tuareg tribesmen (*like the one below*) still meet and trade, much as they did when Europeans first came to the town in the 1820s. ▼

The Niger

In 1795 the Association sent out a 24-year-old Scottish doctor, called Mungo Park. Sensible, courteous, intelligent and brave, he survived many adventures – including four months of imprisonment – to travel 500 kms (300 miles) down the Niger, discovering that it flowed east.

Encouraged, the Association sent him out again, this time to find the mouth of the Niger. He set out from the mouth of the Gambia in 1805 with 40 Europeans. Few survived to reach the Niger, and the last ones – including Park – died before they reached the mouth.

In 1822, the British government sent an expedition to the Kingdom of Bornu on Lake Chad, which might, it was believed, be the source of the Niger. The three leaders – Dixon Denham, Hugh Clapperton and Walter Oudney – were the first Europeans to see the great lake. When Denham and Clapperton returned (Oudney had died), they brought astonishing reports of the African kingdoms beyond the Sahara.

43

The Source of the Nile

A map showing three major expeditions to find the source of the River Nile. ▶

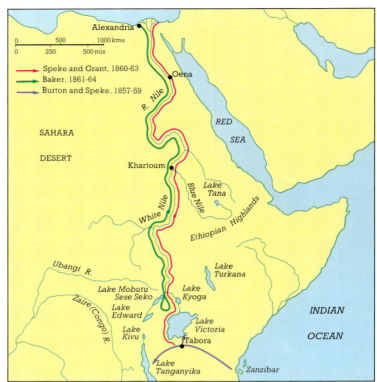

▲ Richard Burton disguised himself as an Afghan in order to penetrate the Moslem holy city of Mecca. He was a handsome, brilliant, daring man who had no respect for authority.

In the middle of the 19th century, the source of the Nile remained unknown. No one knew much more about it than the Greek geographer Ptolemy, who said it rose between Crophi and Mophi, 'The Mountains of the Moon'.

There were reports of two mountains with snow on them (Mount Kilimanjaro and Mount Kenya), which might have been Ptolemy's Mountains of the Moon. In 1856, the Royal Geographical Society decided to find out. The expedition was headed by Richard Burton, an adventurer who was brilliant at languages and at disguise. His companion was John Hanning Speke. Both were officers in the Indian army.

Lake Victoria

In 1857, the two journeyed inland to Ujiji, on the shores of Lake Tanganyika. By now both men were sick. Still, Speke was fit enough to journey on to a great lake to the north, Lake Victoria, which he was sure was the source of the Nile. He then raced Burton home, and broke the news. By the time Burton arrived

back, Speke had another expedition organized to prove his claim, much to Burton's fury.

Speke took with him a less dramatic man named James Grant. Trekking inland from the coast by Zanzibar, Speke and Grant spent some time with the king of Buganda (now part of Uganda). They went on to find the spot where one branch of the Nile flows out of Lake Victoria, and then headed north. They missed discovering that the river flows through another lake – Lake Albert.

Rejoining the Nile at Gondokoro, they had a strange meeting. A friend of Speke's, Samuel Baker and his Hungarian-born wife Florence, had come looking for him, secretly hoping to discover the source of the Nile themselves. The Bakers, in fact, went on to find Lake Albert, and the 36 m (120 feet) Murchison Falls where the Nile drops out of the lake.

The Bakers arrived in London in 1865. Yet the answer to the riddle of the source of the Nile was still not complete. The final details would not emerge for another 24 years.

▲ The Murchison Falls, where the River Nile flows out of Lake Albert.

Up until the nineteenth century people believed that the source of the Nile lay somewhere near Mount Kilimanjaro in Tanzania. ▼

Missionary Explorers

Much of Central Africa was explored and mapped by a Scot, David Livingstone, and the journalist, Henry Morton Stanley. ▶

The Zambezi is as placid as this stretch for most of its journey from central Africa to the east coast. When Livingstone explored it in 1855-6, he reported it offered easy access to the interior. Unfortunately, he missed seeing a major obstacle – the Quebrabasa Rapids. ▼

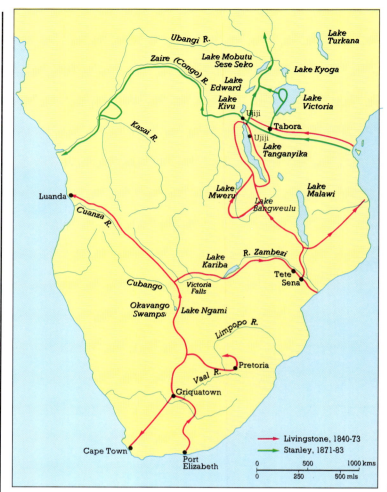

David Livingstone

One of the best known names in the history of exploration was David Livingstone. At 28, he moved from Scotland to South Africa. At the time (1841) nothing was known of the desert lands to the north. Livingstone was the first to cross them, finding a lake, Ngami, where he set up a mission station.

He had a great ambition: to pioneer a highway from the coast into the interior so that slavery could be destroyed. He had tried to do this in the south. Now he went to the west coast, and then crossed back the 3,000 km (2,000 miles) to the east coast, hoping the Zambezi River would be a good route for sailing inland.

When in 1856 he reported back to England, he found himself a hero. The government asked him to lead a huge expedition, but it was a disaster. On his next return to England, he did his best to evade blame and asked for a bigger expedition. This time the government would not listen. Livingstone went back to Africa on his own to preach and campaign against slavery. He ran out of money, and fell ill, cut off in Ujiji on the shores of Lake Tanganyika.

Henry Morton Stanley

His life was saved by a near miracle: the arrival of an American at the head of a large expedition who greeted him with the famous words: 'Dr Livingstone, I presume?' The man was Henry Morton Stanley, raised in a workhouse in Wales and now a journalist on the *New York Herald.* The editor had told him to find Livingstone.

Livingstone recovered and insisted on one last journey: to find the fabled Mountains of the Moon. He said they would prove to be the real source of the Nile. He searched in vain – for he was nowhere near the Nile – fell ill again, and died in 1873, kneeling by his bed, lost in swampland. It was Stanley who completed the exploration of central Africa, with a successful journey the length of the Congo River.

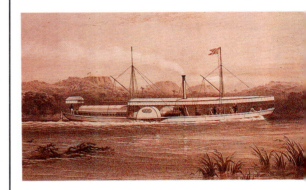

▲ Sailing up the Zambezi in his boat the *Ma Robert* (*above*), Livingstone discovered rapids, and turned north to explore Lake Nyasa. Then, on a final expedition to find the source of the Nile, he became lost. He was found by Stanley (*left*). Livingstone continued the search alone. ▼

9: OPENING THE OUTBACK

Across the Divide

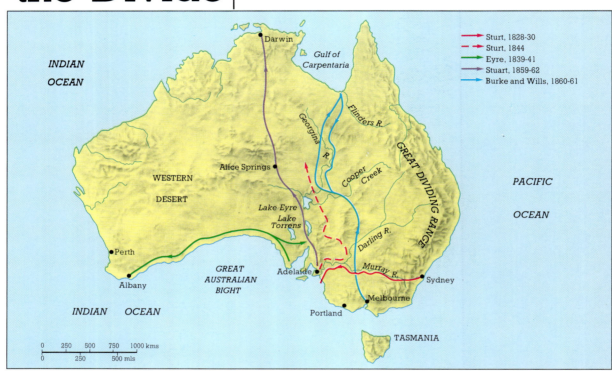

	Sturt, 1828-30
	Sturt, 1844
	Eyre, 1839-41
	Stuart, 1859-62
	Burke and Wills, 1860-61

▲ For many years, the early settlers in Australia did not venture into the desert interior. This map shows the routes of the main expeditions that took place in the nineteenth century to discover what was beyond the 'ghastly blank'.

For 40 years after the first white settlement of Australia in 1788, no one ventured far beyond the Great Dividing Range that stretches for 4,800 km (3,000 miles) up the eastern shore. It was called the 'ghastly blank', known only by the native peoples, the Aborigines.

The Darling River

First to go was Charles Sturt. He was driven inland by the need to find water in this parched land. Having already found that there were rivers to be explored to the west, Sturt and six others set out down the Murrumbidgee in 1829, and floated out into the Murray. They rowed to the Darling River, which took them

48

westwards towards the coast – and then to their horror ended in a lake.

There was nothing for it but to return by rowing 1,600 km (1,000 miles) upstream. As a result of Sturt's report, colonists flocked westward, across what is now Victoria to the present-day port of Adelaide.

Again, attention turned towards the 'ghastly blank' inland to the north. First off the mark was Edward Eyre, who left Adelaide in 1840, aiming for the centre of the continent. For months, he was all but lost in swamp land

◄▲ The gum-forests and 500-foot cliffs of the Blue Mountains (*left*), part of the Great Dividing Range, were a major barrier to explorers. But beyond them, rivers like the Darling (*above*) led to the edge of the desert interior.

▼ Edward Eyre and the Aborigine, Wylie, two survivors from the 1840 expedition into the centre of Australia.

where mirages haunted him. He gave up, and headed west, hoping to find a route along which sheep could be driven. His new plan landed him in an epic journey – 1,600 km (1,000 miles) along the desert coast of the Great Australian Bight. There is not a single river in the whole stretch.

At a point not even half way, two of the guides killed Eyre's servant and ran away with the stores. He was left with one loyal Aborigine, Wylie. The two survived by eating their horse and by seeking help from a French ship at anchor near the coast. After more weeks of travel, Eyre and Wylie reached Albany, almost on the west coast, to end one of the greatest journeys of Australian exploration.

The Simpson Desert

Charles Sturt starts off northwards from Adelaide in 1844. He was hoping to find a great inland sea. Instead he saw ridge upon ridge of impenetrable spiky, spinifex grass, and turned back in despair. ▶

Burke was brave, but had no experience of the Outback. He also had a violent temper that turned his men against him. ▼

Into the Interior

Charles Sturt still believed there was a great inland sea and set off north from Adelaide in 1844 to find it. His was a great expedition of 15 men, 11 horses, 200 sheep and 30 bullocks. After enduring heat up to 55° C (132° F) in the shade and crossing a desert of 15 cm (6 ins) flints, he entered the Simpson Desert. One look at the endless waves of red rock and sand was enough: he gave up.

The Telegraph

When the government wanted to link north and south by **telegraph** (1859) it offered £2,000 to the first person who made the crossing. Two

rival expeditions were formed, one headed by a Scot, John Stuart, the second by an Irishman, Robert Burke.

Stuart reached further north than any European before him. He passed what is now Alice Springs and marked the centre of the continent by naming a hill Central Mount Sturt 'after the Father of Australian Exploration'. It was later renamed Stuart after its discoverer. He never completed his journey, being forced to turn back by lack of food 500 km (300 miles) from the north coast.

Burke's expedition, meanwhile, was on its way to tragedy. Burke first divided his party

into two, leaving the supplies to follow in the second group. While waiting at a river called Cooper Creek for the second group to catch up, he divided his men again, leaving some behind to meet the supplies, while he and three other men went ahead. Finally, he accused two of his men of going too slowly and left them behind while he and his second-in-command, William Wills, raced on ahead to the north coast.

When the four returned to Cooper Creek, the place was deserted. A note revealed what had happened. The supplies had never arrived. Despairing, those left behind at Cooper Creek had headed for home just a few hours before Burke's arrival. For some reason, Burke decided he would never be able to catch them up, and headed off in another direction. Incredibly, both teams then returned to Cooper Creek, but missed each other. All but one died in the desert. The survivor, John King, was found wandering three months later, a walking skeleton kept alive by curious Aborigines.

The Burke and Wills expeditions were the first to use camels in this land. Some of the animals escaped and still breed wild in the Outback.

▲ Cooper Creek was the meeting point for the Burke and Wills expedition that made the first crossing of Australia. It was near here that most of them died, victims of deserts like the one below. Early explorers like Burke and Wills introduced camels into Australia because they took to desert conditions better than horses. Now they are a common sight in the Outback. The desert shown here is the Strzelecki Desert, about 16 days march south of Cooper Creek. ▼

10: | THE ENDS OF THE EARTH

The North Pole

A map showing the main expeditionary routes in the Arctic. ▶

An Inuit (Eskimo) family. These people have adapted to the severe and monotonous Arctic conditions of Greenland and Northern Canada. ▼

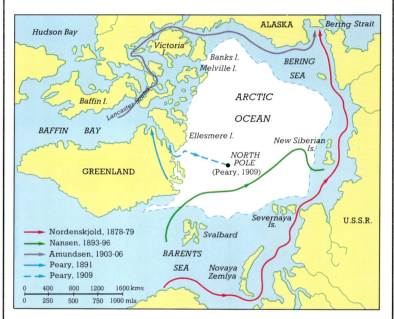

Nordenskjold, 1878-79
Nansen, 1893-96
Amundsen, 1903-06
Peary, 1891
Peary, 1909

The North Pole has always drawn people, probably because it is quite close to so much of Northern Europe, America and Asia.

In the 19th century, the British remained as interested in the Northwest Passage as the early explorers had been, this time to stop Russia getting there first. In 1818, Commander John Ross probed Lancaster Sound, which was the right way westwards, except that he turned back because he thought he saw mountains blocking his way.

The next year, another expedition under Edward Parry proved there were no mountains blocking Lancaster Sound. Parry reached Melville Island, half way to the Bering Strait, before winter – bringing ice 2 m (7 ft) thick and temperatures of −50° C – locked him in. He returned home in the spring.

◀ The first man to cross the polar ice cap on foot was the British explorer Wally Herbert, seen here (*right*); with other polar explorers.

Discovering Magnetic North

John Ross headed another expedition in 1829, during which he discovered the Magnetic North Pole. After three years in the Arctic, Ross's ship had to be abandoned. He and his men survived the winter by building a house, and were then lucky enough to be picked up by a whaler.

Locked in Ice

The next attempt to reach the Bering Strait came in 1845. The commander was Sir John Franklin. The Franklin expedition sailed away into legend, because it vanished completely. It took 14 years and many searches to find out what happened. A written note and Inuit accounts told the story. Franklin's ships had become locked in the ice. Franklin and many others died on board of scurvy and other diseases. After 18 months, the survivors had abandoned ship. The Inuit who had seen them tottering across the ice disfigured by disease said they died as they walked.

Strangely, the Northeast Passage, from northern Sweden across the top of Russia, was sailed before the Northwest Passage – by a Swede, Baron Nordenskjöld, in 1878-9. The Northwest Passage was finally navigated in 1903-6 by the Norwegian, Roald Amundsen.

Nansen

One way to the Pole itself was devised by the Norwegian Fridtjof Nansen in 1893-6. This expert Arctic traveller invented a special lightweight **sled** and also designed a ship with a specially shaped hull that would slip up out of the ice if it closed in. Aware of the Arctic currents, Nansen allowed his ship to join the slowly moving pack ice for a three-year drift around and towards the Pole. Then in sleds and kayaks, he headed north, getting to a point 386 km (240 miles) from the Pole.

Fridtjof Nansen was not just a great explorer – he was a brilliant scientist. He was a professor twice over, first of zoology then oceanography. He also drew fine illustrations for his accounts of his own travels. ▼

The South Pole

A map of the main expeditionary routes in search of the South Pole. ▶

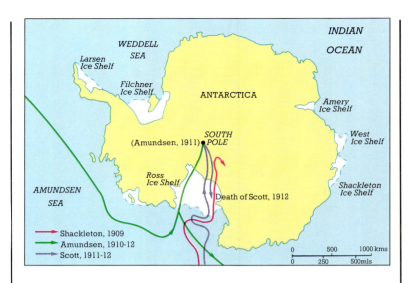

▲ Robert Scott writes up his diary at Camp Evans before beginning his ill-fated journey to the South Pole.

Camping out in Antarctica is a grim business. High winds whip snow into a fog-like 'white out', and bitter cold can freeze exposed flesh in less than a minute. ▶

The continent at the South Pole is called Antarctica and the first landing on it had been made in 1895. In the first years of the century several nations sent expeditions. One (1901-04) was made by the British under a naval lieutenant, Robert Scott, who spent two winters there on the Ross Ice Shelf, a frozen inlet 650 km (400 miles) deep.

Ernest Shackleton

In 1908, Ernest Shackleton who had been a member of Scott's party, set up a base on the coast. When spring came, he and three others

set off for the Pole, 1,300 km (800 miles) away. Climbing up from the coast, he discovered a huge glacier, the Beardmore, 160 km (100 miles) long, leading to the 3,000 m (10,000 feet) highlands of the interior. They made it to within 160 km (100 miles) but ran short of food and had to turn back.

Scott and Amundsen

The stage was now set for the race to the Pole. It was between two very different men: Scott and the Norwegian Roald Amundsen. Amundsen already knew all about Inuit ways of survival; his Arctic furs were half the weight of Scott's clothing, he was used to handling dogs, and was ready to kill and eat them if necessary. This Scott would not do. He had 33 men, 33 dogs and 17 ponies. Amundsen had eight men and 118 dogs.

Amundsen made the trip in seven weeks. His team stayed at the Pole for three days, leaving behind them a small tent, and returned in just over a month, 'men and animals all hale and hearty'.

Scott set off with motor-sledges, ponies and dogs, but the expedition soon ran into trouble. For example, the sledges soon broke down. Scott and four companions prepared to drag their own supplies the remaining 286 km (178 miles) to the Pole. After an 18-day march, they made it, only to find Amundsen's tent.

▲ The wrinkled surface of the Beardmore Glacier offers one of the best routes inland.

Shackleton's base hut from his 1907-9 expedition. ▼

The Bitter End

Exhausted and disappointed, Scott and his men turned around to walk back to their base camp, 300 km (200 miles) away. The weather worsened. One of the team, Edgar Evans, died on the Beardmore Glacier. Another, Lawrence Oates, realizing that there was not enough food for them all, sacrificed his own life in the hope that the others would survive. He left the tent saying, 'I'm just going outside and may be some time.' He was never seen again. The remaining three froze to death 12 days later. Scott's last thoughts, recorded in his journal, were for their families: 'For God's sake look after our people.'

◄ Roald Amundsen hoists the Norwegian flag over the South Pole.

The Last Unknown

Ernest Shackleton had his ship, the *Endurance*, locked in ice for nine months. ▶

Essential to survival in the freezing cold of the Arctic or Antarctic is the proper clothing. ▼

Balaclava hat

Padded snow-jacket

Lined gloves

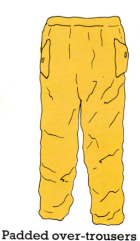

Padded over-trousers

Snow boots

There were many other heroic journeys in the Antarctic in the early years of this century. Shackleton, for instance, returned in 1915 to cross the continent. His ship, the *Endurance* was caught in the ice, and carried helplessly for nine months. Then the ice began to crush the ship. Shackleton ordered his crew of 28 to abandon her, lowering life-boats and stores to the ice.

For four months they drifted on the ice. When the ice began to break up they were able to launch the small boats and land on Elephant Island. They were still 800 miles from their base. Shackleton led a small party to the camp and eventually all his men were saved.

Mapping and Photographing

Air travel has changed Antarctic exploration into something less heroic and more scientific. Rival nations laid claim to various parts of Antarctica, and backed huge research expedi-

tions. In 1946-7, the USA sent 5,000 men in 13 ships to map 900,000 sq. km (350,000 sq. miles) and photograph over half the 4,500 km (2,800 miles) of coast. In 1957, a British expedition led by Sir Vivian Fuchs crossed the continent in powerful tracked Snocats. As a result of this scientific exploration, a huge amount was learned about Antarctica. For instance, its ice, which averages 2.5 km (8,000 ft) thick, holds as much water as the Atlantic Ocean.

The 12 Nation Treaty

By the end of the 1950s, 12 nations had laid claims to land there. In the past, wars were fought over such claims. But so successful was the research that the 12 nations all signed a treaty promising to use Antarctica for peaceful purposes only for the next 30 years (until 1989). There is much more to be explored by scientists, and the chances are that research will continue in peace.

▲ Modern Antarctic research is made safer and easier by the use of ice-breakers like this.

Frontiers of the Future

The great days of geographical exploration are over, of course. Now that the whole earth can be photographed by **satellites**, there is no need for men to toil over deserts and hack through jungles just to find out what is there. Many dangerous places can be explored by a machine. A **submersible** has even reached the deepest ocean floor, 11 km (7 miles) down in the Mariana Trench in the Pacific.

New Challenges

There are still some challenges for explorers. For example, there is a cave in France 1,120 m (3,680 ft) deep, and another in Switzerland 60 km (37 miles) long. There are uncounted miles of caves still to explore, and much to be learned in doing so. Cave explorers need all the courage, and more expertise, than any old fashioned explorer. Underwater caving is one of the most dangerous activities there is.

And there are still discoveries to be made in the world's rainforests. The Amazon still con-

▲ The depths of the world's oceans are still largely a mystery. This submersible has been specially designed to withstand the great pressure of water when exploring the ocean floor.

Exploration in space is the next great challenge for the human race. Here we see an artist's impression of people colonizing the moon and exploring its surface. There will be other planets further away, for us to find out about. ▶

tains tribes little known to the outside world. There are still plants with unknown chemical properties many of which may be of use to people. And there are species of animals unrecorded that are living testament to the great variety of life on earth.

Exploring Space

Space is often called the last frontier. It always will be, because it is a frontier without end. But (so far at least) it is a very different frontier for explorers. Astronauts know where they are going and their journeys are carefully planned. Mistakes are very costly, because the astronauts are in entirely hostile surroundings and thousands of people have spent a great deal of money getting them there. A hundred years ago, usually if an explorer died no one but his family and friends suffered. Today, the eyes of nations are on the individuals who explore space. We are all aware of the dangers that they face.

▲ Christian Bonington uses his computer to record his notes. This famous British mountaineer has led many expeditions in the Himalayas and other mountain ranges.

This man is pot-holing in the Pyrenees in France. This is a dangerous sport but an exciting one. ▼

Glossary

Amazons: in Greek mythology, a nation of women warriors.

Amazon basin: the area that is drained by the Amazon River and all the smaller rivers that flow into the Amazon.

Botanist: a scientist who studies plants.

Campaign: a military journey in which a general and his army venture into countries to make conquests.

Civilisation: a nation or group of nations that have reached a stage in their development that frees them from mere survival so that they can devote energy to music, poetry, art and philosophical debate.

Compass: an instrument that contains a floating magnetic needle which always points to magnetic north. It is used in finding the direction.

Convict: someone who has done something wrong and has been or will be punished for it, a criminal.

Cossacks: people who originally came from south-eastern Russia, known for their great horsemanship and cavalry expertise.

Currach: an Irish word, meaning a small long-shaped boat used for rowing. They are made by stretching skins or tarred canvas over a wooden frame.

Equator: an imaginary circle around the Earth, lying halfway between the North and South Poles.

Expedition: a journey that is usually well-organised and has a purpose (for example, military or scientific).

Frankincense: a gum-like substance that comes from trees. It has a beautiful smell and is used as incense.

Galleon: a large sailing ship of the 16th century. It was used by the Spanish.

Geographer: someone who studies geography, or the science of the Earth (its surface, physical features, products and populations).

Great Barrier Reef: a reef is a ridge of rock, sand or coral just below the level of the water. The Great Barrier Reef is found off the east coast of Australia and is 2000 km (1,250 miles) long. It is made of coral.

Great Khan: this was the title given to the medieval emperors of central Asia.

Hides: the skins of animals, often used by people as covering or clothing.

Humidity: the amount of water vapour in the air. A large amount leads to dampness and unpleasant conditions.

Ice Age: a period in Earth's history characterised by severe cold and the spread of glaciers.

Interpreter: someone who can speak and write in more than one language and is employed to do so for the benefit of those who cannot.

Inuit: a member of the peoples native to Canada and Greenland, once known as Eskimos.

Jesuit: a member of the Roman Catholic religious order, called the Society of Jesus.

Junk: a flat-bottomed Chinese sailing ship.

Kayak: a canoe, first used by the Inuit (Eskimos) of North America and Greenland.

Longitude: an east or west position. Lines of longitude are imaginary lines that run around the Earth from North to South Pole.

Malaria: a type of fever that can make people seriously ill. It is carried by the female mosquito. People may become infected if these mosquitos bite them.

Manslaughter: the unlawful but unintentional killing of another person, for example, by driving recklessly.

Mecca: a city in Saudi Arabia, where Mohammed, the prophet of Islam, was born. It is a holy place and centre of pilgrimage for many Muslims.

Merchant: someone who lives by trading. This is usually on a large scale and includes trading with foreign countries.

Missionary: someone who actively tries to convert people to his or her religion.

Muslim: someone who is a follower of the faith of Islam, founded by the prophet Mohammed.

Mutiny: a revolt against authority. The word is used most often in reference to a military revolt.

Myrrh: a gum used in perfumes and incense.

Navigation: the science of steering a vessel in the right direction, using the stars and special instruments.

Pilgrim: someone who travels to sacred places to worship.

Roc: an extremely large bird that is spoken about in legends but which does not exist today.

Satellite: something that rotates around a larger object. This might be something natural (like the Moon orbiting the Earth) or man-made.

Scurvy: a disease caused by a lack of vitamin C, which is found in fresh fruit and vegetables. People on long sea voyages were once very vulnerable to this disease, because their diet was lacking these foods.

Shoshoni: a North American Indian tribe.

Silk: a fine thread made by a certain type of moth. It is used by people to make beautiful and expensive fabrics.

Sled: a vehicle that moves on runners, designed for use on snow and ice. A larger version is known as a sledge.

Smock: a baggy garment worn as protective clothing. Today it is sometimes used by painters and farmers.

Species: a group, either of plants or animals, the members of which are similar to each other and breed together.

Submersible: a vehicle that can be lowered underwater to great depths. Scientists and marine biologists use them to study life in the seas and oceans.

Telegraph: a method of sending messages using electric signals sent through wires.

Tropics: two imaginary lines around the Earth, running east-west. One is north of the Equator (the Tropic of Cancer), the other is south (the Tropic of Capricorn).

Valet: a manservant; someone employed to take care of the possessions of another person.

Yurt: a type of large tent used by nomadic peoples.

Zoology: the study of animals and the animal kingdom.

Index

A **Bold** number shows the entry is illustrated on that page. The same page often has writing about the entry too.